# RESOURCES

# TEXTILES
## AND THE ENVIRONMENT

## KATHRYN WHYMAN

Franklin Watts
London • Sydney

© Archon Press Ltd 2003

Produced by
Archon Press Ltd
28 Percy Street
London W1T 2BZ

New edition first published in
Great Britain in 2003 by
Franklin Watts
96 Leonard Street
London EC2A 4XD

Original edition published as
Resources Today – Textiles

ISBN 0-7496-4974-7

A CIP record for this
book is available from the
British Library

Printed in UAE

All rights reserved

Editor:
Katie Harker

Designer:
Flick, Book Design & Graphics

Illustrator:
Louise Nevett
Simon Bishop

Picture Researcher:
Brian Hunter Smart

**Photocredits** Abbreviations: l-left, r-right, b-bottom, t-top, c-centre, m-middle.  Front cover main, 16tr — Flick Smith. front cover mt, 6b — John Deere. front cover mb — Flat Earth. 1 — Corel. 2-3 — Corbis Roylaty Free. 4tl, 4b, 5tr, 6tl, 8tl, 10tl, 10b, 12tl, 14tl, 14b, 16tl, 17 both, 18tl, 20tl, 20b, 21b, 22tl, 22br, 24tl, 26tl, 28tl, 30t, 31t, 32t — Corel. 4tr — Roger Vlitos. 5b —  U.S. Navy photo by Chief Photographer's Mate Chris Desmond. 6tr, 7 both — USDA. 8tr, 8-9, 9tr, 14tr, 20tr, 22tr, 23b — Corbis. 10tr — Ingram Publishing. 11 both — G & P Corrigan. 15br — Hutchison Library. 18tr — Robert Harding. 18b — Photodisc. 19t — George Haling/Science Photo Library.

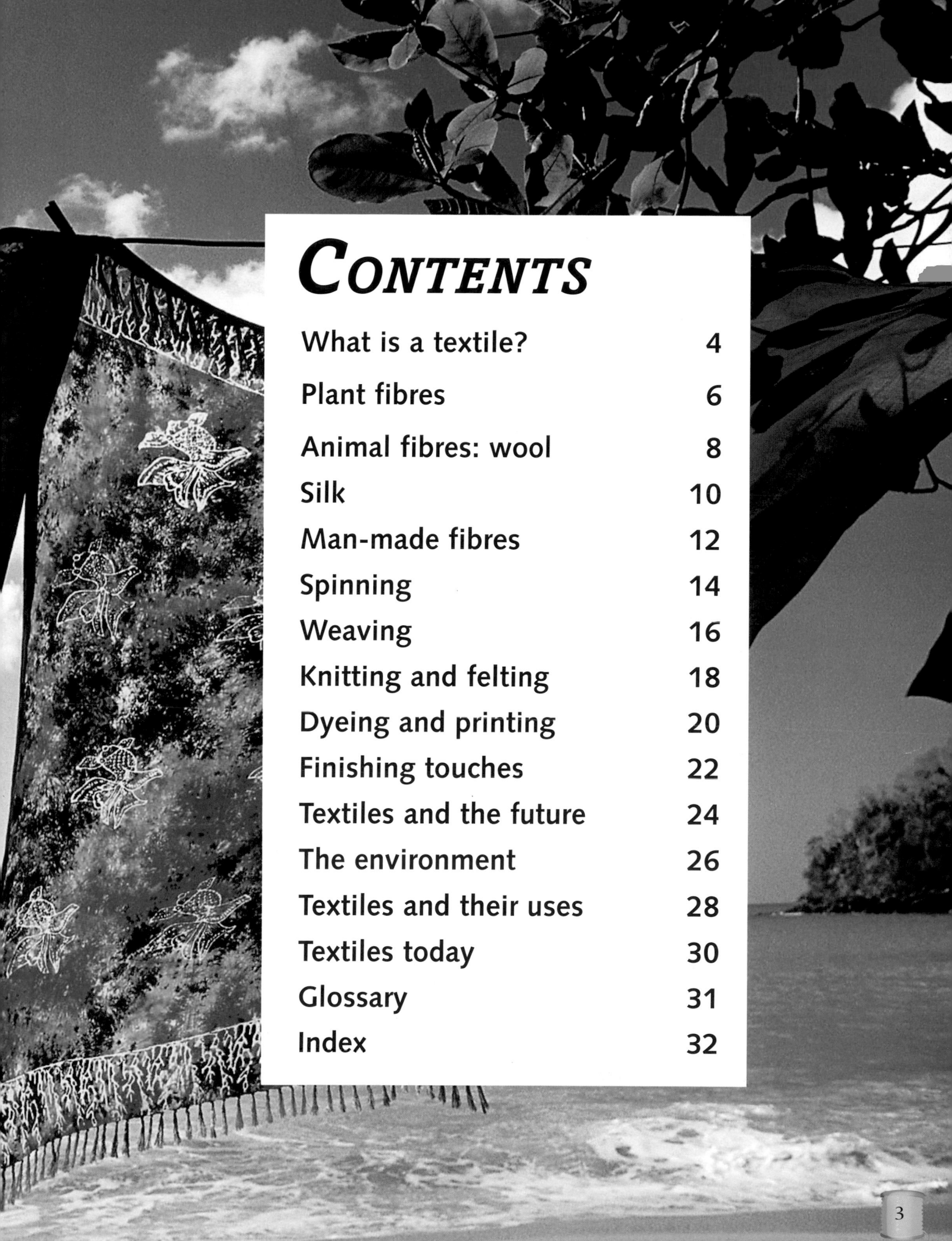

# CONTENTS

# WHAT IS A TEXTILE?

A textile was originally a woven fabric. But today the word describes anything which is manufactured from fibres or yarns (fibres which have been spun together). Cords, ropes, lace and nets are all textiles. Cloths made by weaving, knitting or felting are also textiles. The fibres used in textiles come from either natural or man-made sources. Cotton and wool are examples of natural fibres. Polyester, nylon and Kevlar are fibres that have been man-made from fossil fuels such as oil.

Wool is a natural fibre. It can be dyed to make textiles of different colours.

You only have to look around you to see how important textiles are – from clothes and curtains to carpets and upholstery. There are many industrial uses of textiles too – string, tents and parachutes are a few examples. Textiles are also used to make parts for cars, planes and spacecraft.

Whilst polyester and nylon are made from resources that will eventually run out, plant and animal fibres are made from renewable resources.

A sari made from dyed cotton

This parachute is made from nylon – a man-made fibre.

# PLANT FIBRES

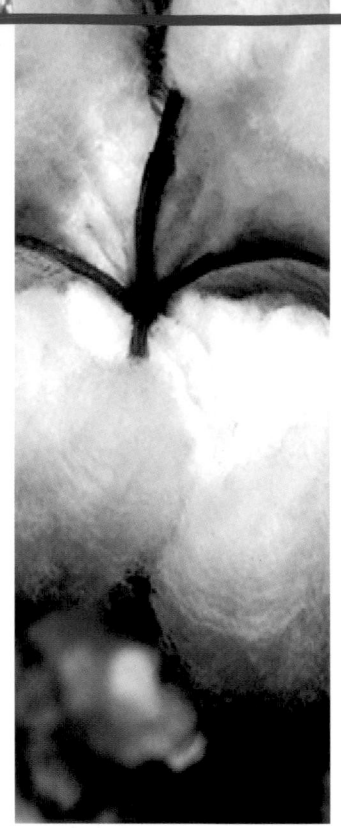

Plant fibres are used extensively to make textiles. These include flax for linen, cotton for t-shirts, sheets and underwear, and jute, sisal, kapok and hemp for rough cloth, sacking and ropes.

Of these, cotton is the most widely used plant fibre. Cotton grows as clumps of soft, white fibres (called bolls) attached to the seeds of the cotton plant. Once harvested, cotton undergoes a process called 'ginning' to separate the fibres. Cotton is now grown mainly in the USA, where a genetically modified crop has reduced the need for insecticides and fertilisers.

Today, most cotton harvesting is a mechanical process.

# Ginning cotton

The harvested cotton is first fed onto a revolving beater (1). Here the leaves and dirt – known as trash – are beaten free from the fibres. A blast of air then blows the fibres onto the rough surface of a large revolving toothed cylinder (the gin) where the teeth catch the fibres and pull them from the seeds (2). The cotton seeds fall into a separate trough for use as cattle food or for vegetable oils (3). Another blast of air then blows the separated fibres from the gin (4) where they are collected ready for spinning (see page 15).

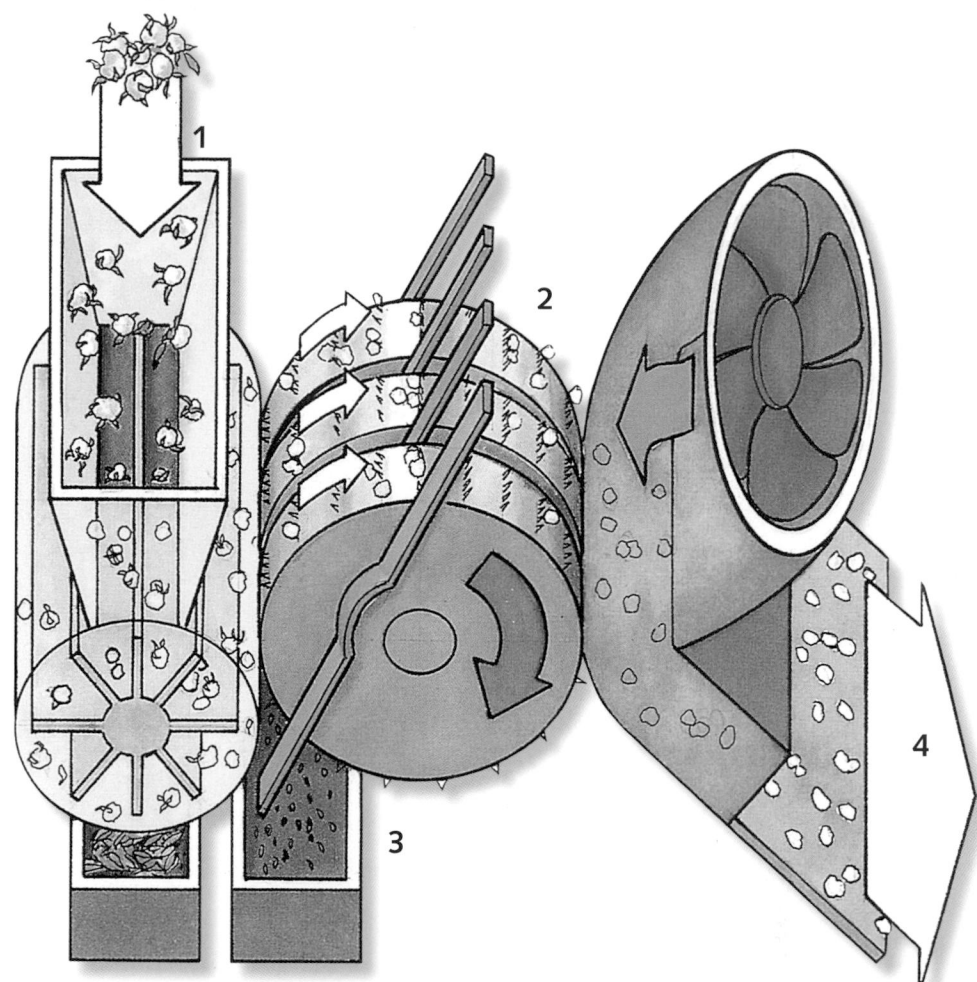

Large bales of cotton fibres arrive at the cotton factory, to be processed for spinning.

# ANIMAL FIBRES: WOOL

Most of the wool we use comes from sheep. When the sheep's coat (the fleece) is removed it is usually very dirty and coated in lanolin – a natural grease produced by the sheep to keep itself warm. Both the dirt and the lanolin have to be removed by sorting and washing. During a process called scouring, the wool is passed through warm baths containing chemicals which dissolve the dirt. It is then rinsed and dried.

By this time the wool is very tangled. All the fibres face in different directions, so the wool has to be fed through a carding machine. This combs through the fibres, arranging them in the same direction (see page 15).

Sheep are reared around the world for their wool, as well as for meat, milk and cheese.

## Sheep shearing

Farmers usually shear (cut away) a sheep's fleece in the spring. The fleece grows back again during the winter months. Electric or hand shears are used to remove the fleece in one piece.

Different breeds of sheep provide different types of wool. Coarse wool is used to make woollen yarn for items such as carpets or thick sweaters. Fine wool is used to make worsted yarn for lighter clothes such as suits or dresses. Lambswool is a soft wool from the first shearing of a lamb, when it is about seven months old.

Wool has many useful characteristics. It is warm to wear, stretches and can absorb water without feeling wet. Most of our wool comes from sheep but smaller quantities also come from other animals, like goats and camels (below).

Bactrian camel

Alpaca

Cashmere goat

Merino sheep

Angora goat

Karakui sheep

# SILK

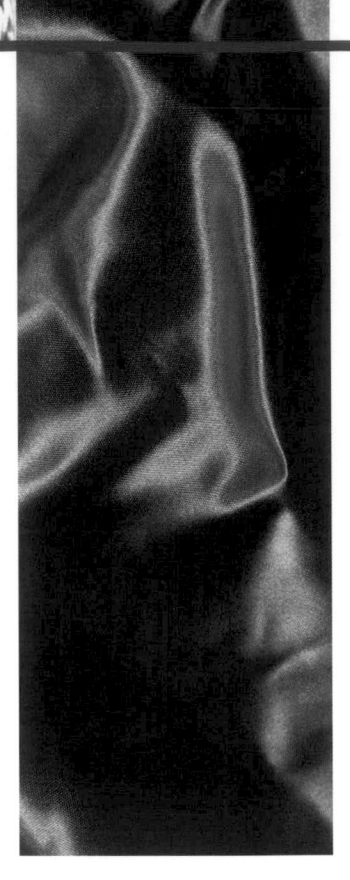

Silk is a strong, smooth and very valuable fabric, first made in China about 2600 BC. It has a beautiful natural luster and is more elastic than cotton or linen.

Silkworms spin a cocoon of thread which can be up to 1,000 metres long! Once killed by heat, their cocoons are treated to soften the natural gum that binds the fine threads together. The silk threads are unwound by machine and twisted together to form a yarn strong enough to be woven or knitted. It is an extraordinary story that still today, millions of silkworms are sacrificed to make luxury items such as dresses, gloves and scarves.

10 Silk is woven on specialised looms. Some of the finest silk fabrics are still woven by hand.

## The silkworm

The adult silkworm moth (1) lays its eggs on mulberry leaves. Silkworm caterpillars hatch from these eggs and start to feed on the leaves (2). They eat for 30 days and moult four times before they start to spin a coccon (3). The silkworm produces silk thread from two tiny holes below its mouth called spinnerets. It spins for two or three days until it is encased (4). Adult moths emerge from the cocoons but on a silk farm most silkworms are killed in their cocoons for their silk threads.

Chinese silkworms (left) make high quality silk.

Silk threads are unwound from silkworm cocoons using a machine called a filature.

# MAN-MADE FIBRES

Although man-made, the first artificial fibres were made from natural substances. These artificial fibres (known as rayons) are made from cellulose, a substance found in wood and other plants. Used extensively today – from clothing to vehicle parts – these artificial fibres are made from renewable resources.

Nylon was first invented in 1938 using a mix of chemicals, and was an instant success for clothing and industrial uses. Today there is a wide range of artificial fibres also made from chemicals found in coal, oil and gas. But these fibres rely on the precious use of non-renewable fossil fuels.

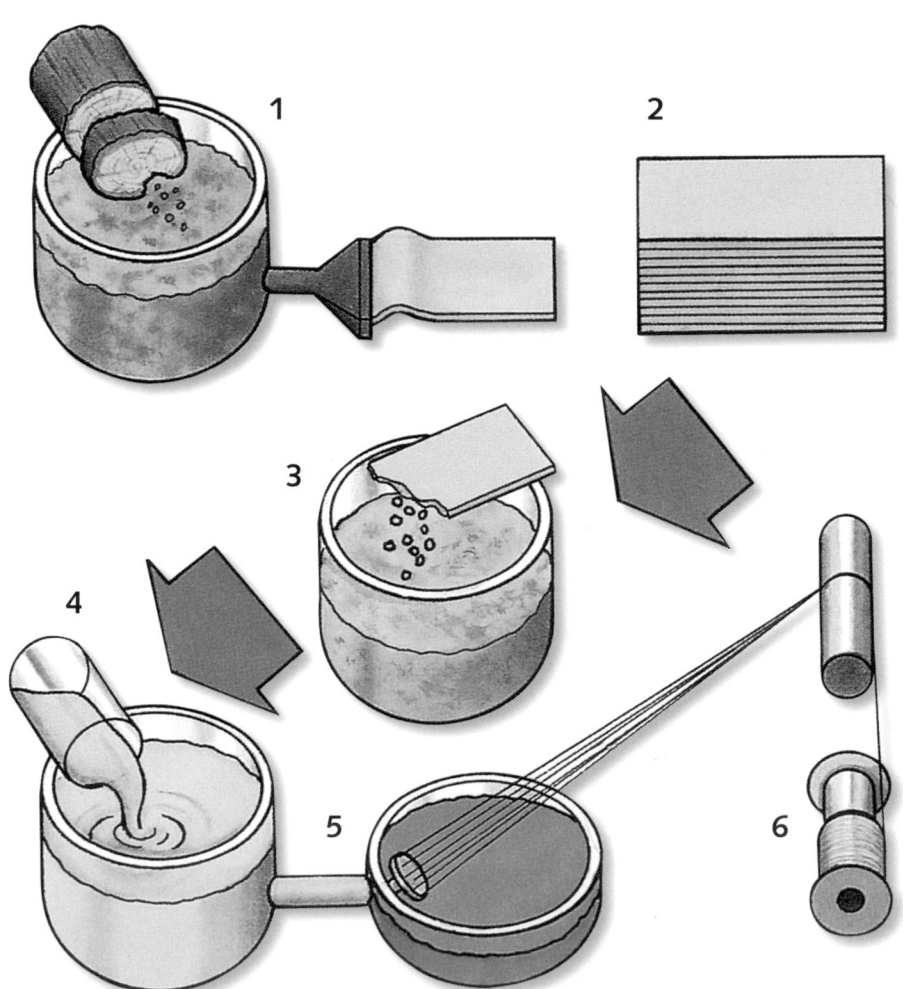

## Viscose rayon

Viscose rayon is made from the cellulose in wood. The wood is mixed with water and a chemical called caustic soda (1). This dissolves the cellulose fibres which are then extracted, made into cellulose sheets (2) and mixed with another chemical, carbon disulphide (3). When this mixture is left to soak in a bath of caustic soda for a few days (4), it forms a syrupy liquid. The liquid is squirted through a spinneret (a nozzle full of tiny holes), and emersed in sulphuric acid (5). The acid solidifies the liquid into long, thin fibres of viscose rayon (6).

## Nylon

Nylon is made from chemicals which are found in oil. When the chemicals are heated (1) they form a liquid which is made up of very long molecules called polymers. The liquid is forced through a spinneret and cooled (2) so that the polymers harden into a series of filaments. These are wound onto a spool (3) and then fed through a series of rollers (4). The filaments are stretched by the rollers before being wound onto a spinning bobbin (5). The long filaments are then chopped up to make short fibres of nylon.

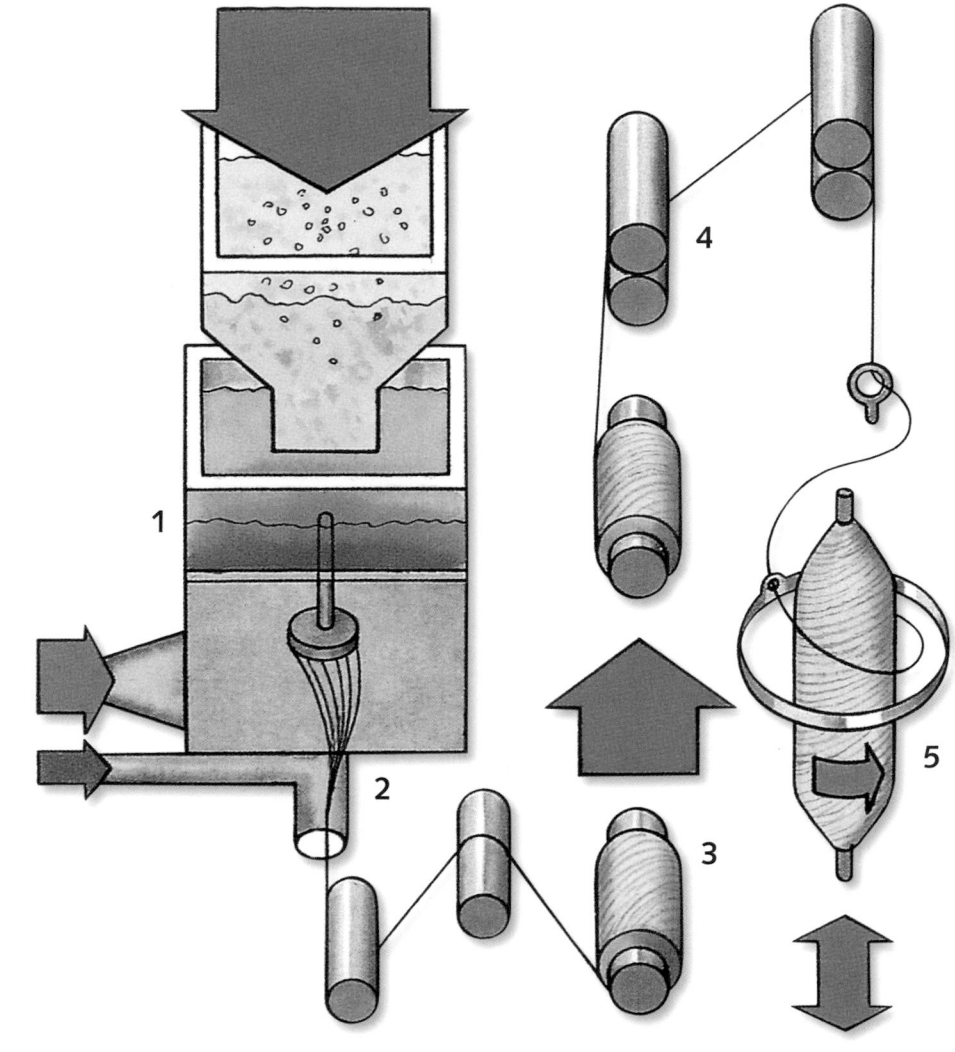

Some waterproof clothes are made from man-made fibres (left).

A spinneret showing man-made fibres hardening

# SPINNING

Most natural fibres like wool and cotton are short and weak. They have to be spun into stronger, longer yarns before they can be used to make textiles. Often the fibres are still dirty and tangled when they arrive at the spinning mill. They have to be cleaned and combed.

After cleaning, the ropes of untangled fibres (called slivers) are stretched by rollers so that the threads lie in the same direction. The fibres are then twisted slightly to form a yarn called roving. This yarn is spun further so that the short fibres overlap and twist together. After spinning, the intertwined fibres cannot slide past each other – they form a long, strong thread or yarn.

The art of spinning has been around for thousands of years.

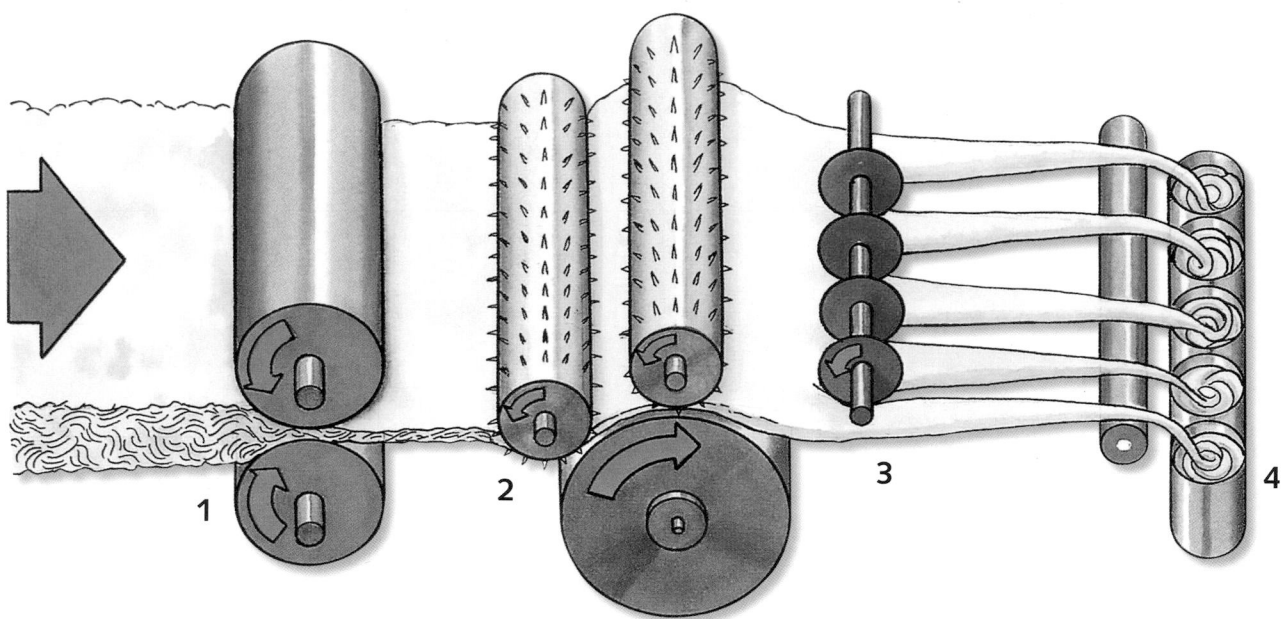

## Carding cotton

The first rollers (1) squeeze the fibres together into a mat which is fed onto wire-toothed rollers (2). These rollers comb out the tangled fibres.

A number of vertical rollers (3) divide the sections called slivers. The slivers are collected in sliver bins (4) where they wait for the next stage.

## Drawing and roving

Several slivers are stretched between slowly rotating rollers (1) to straighten the fibres and twist them into a single roving, wound onto a bobbin (2).

## Spinning

Yet more rollers stretch the roving and twist it into a finer and finer thread (3). The spinning process is now complete and the final thread is collected on a bobbin (4).

Slivers being stretched and twisted into rovings.

# WEAVING

Weaving is the main process that converts yarns – both natural and artificial – into jackets, skirts and other items of fabric around us. These cloths are made up of warp threads (which run lengthways) and weft threads (which run widthways). In the simplest woven fabric, weft threads pass over and under the warp threads.

Although weaving was probably originally used to make baskets and mats from reeds and other plant stems, there is evidence to suggest that simple hand looms were used in 3000 BC in North Africa and Europe. Today textiles are mainly woven on automated looms which allow a great variety of design and weave patterns.

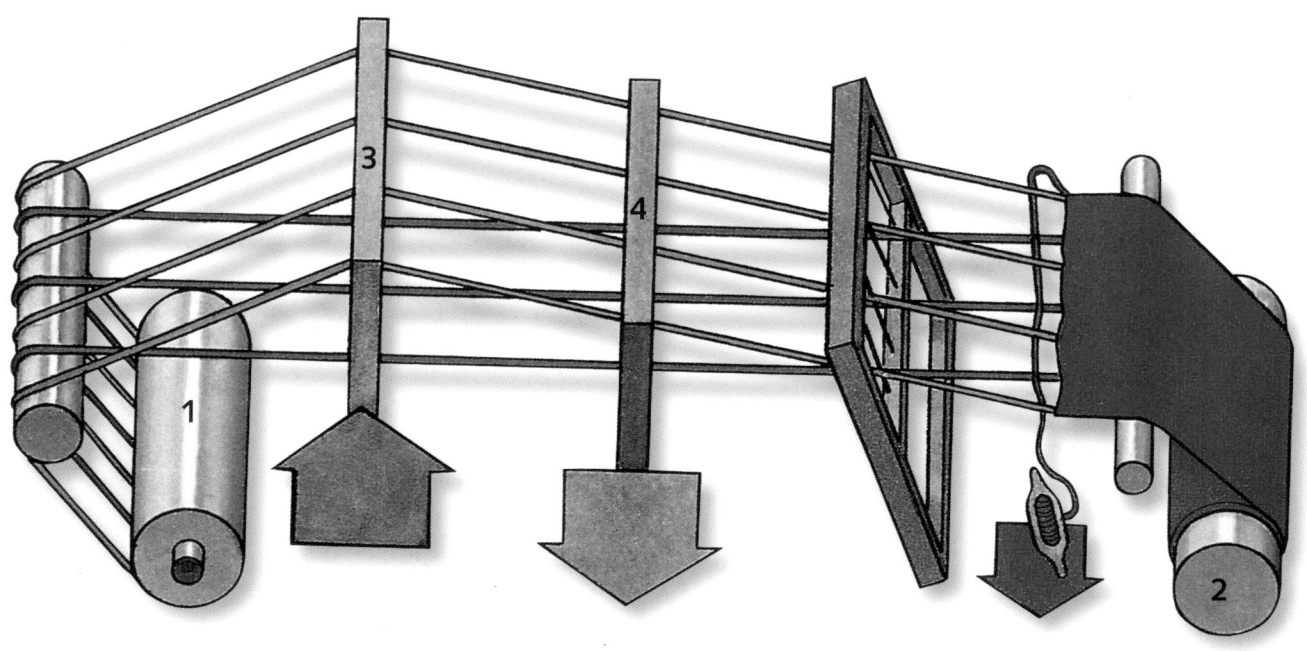

## The loom

This diagram shows how a simple loom works. The warp threads are unwound from the warp beam (1) and stretch along the length of the loom to the cloth beam at the other end (2). Alternate warp threads pass through the back shaft (3) while the rest are threaded through the front shaft (4). When the front and back shafts are raised or lowered, a gap forms between the warp threads.

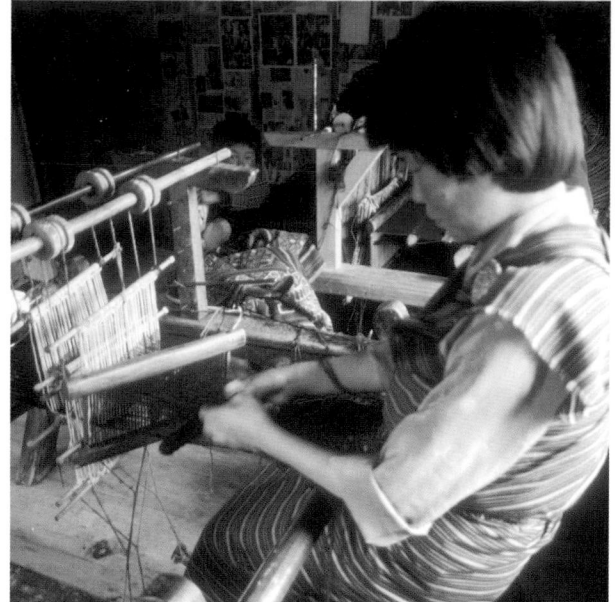

Hand looms are still used to weave some materials.

## Making fabric

The weft thread is carried by a shuttle (5). The shuttle passes through the gap in the warp threads. When the shafts change position the shuttle returns again ready to repeat the process. The reed (6) pushes the weft threads tightly down on the developing cloth. As the process is repeated again and again, the newly-formed cloth is wound onto the cloth beam.

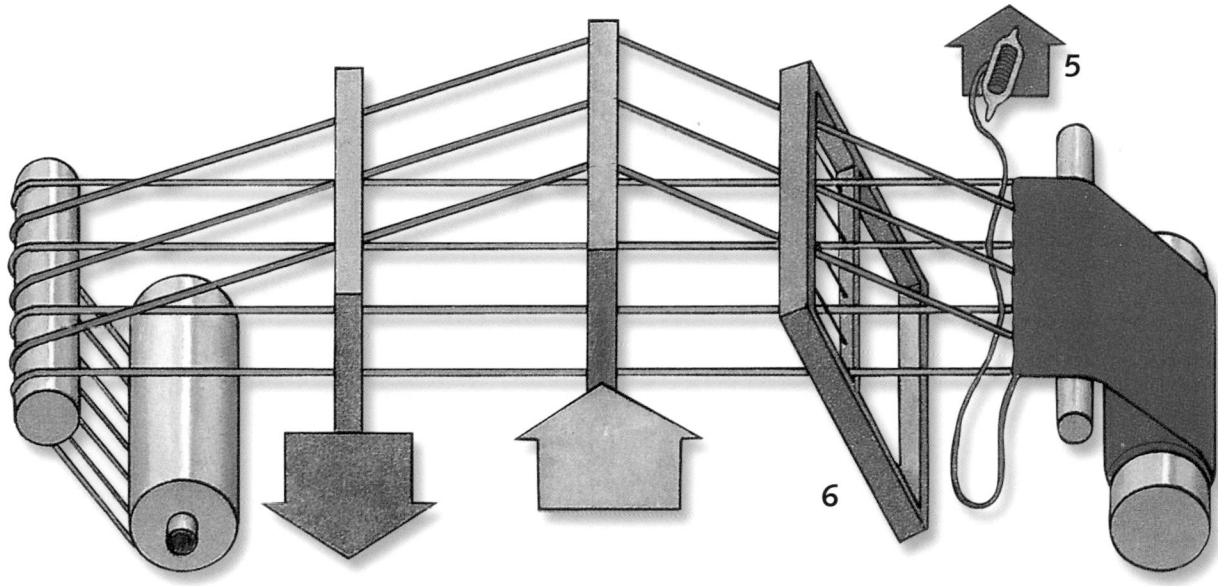

The art of weaving has been practised around the world throughout history. For centuries people have used woven materials to protect themselves from the cold, to warm stone flooring or to provide decoration in the home. Over the years, different cultures have developed their own styles, colours and patterns. Sometimes, rugs are made from recycled materials – using old rags as the weft and warp threads.

Decorative rugs from South America.

# KNITTING AND FELTING

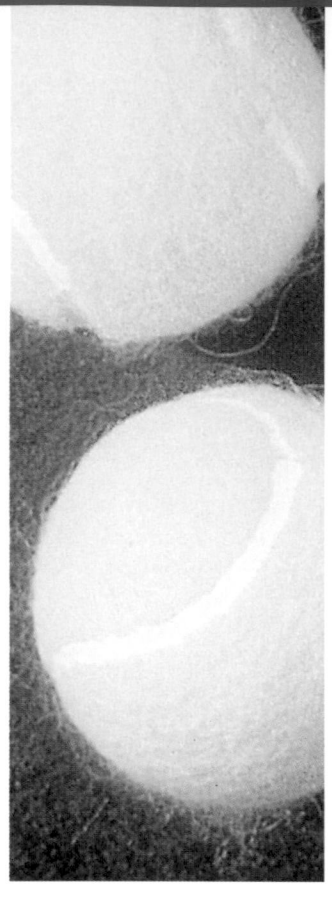

Knitting is another way of turning yarns into fabrics. Knitting links one or more yarns together by loops or stitches. Knitted fabrics are looser and stretchier than woven fabrics, and include jumpers, scarves and socks.

There are two main types of knitting. Weft knitting is used to make clothes. This type of knitting uses one continuous length of yarn to make loops across the width of the fabric. Weft knitting can be done by hand (using knitting needles) or by machine. Warp knitting is used to make fabrics for upholstery and carpets. It uses more than one length of yarn to create different patterns.

## Felt

Felt is a compact fabric made from wet woollen fibres which have a natural tendency to cling together because of their scaly surface. First the wet fibres are tangled together. Then they are heated before being pressed together to allow the fibres to shrink. The tangled fibres form a dense matt cloth which can be easily cut in pieces of different shapes. This cloth can be dyed and is suitable for making hats and covering tennis balls. Pool tables are usually covered with a thin layer of green or blue felt (right).

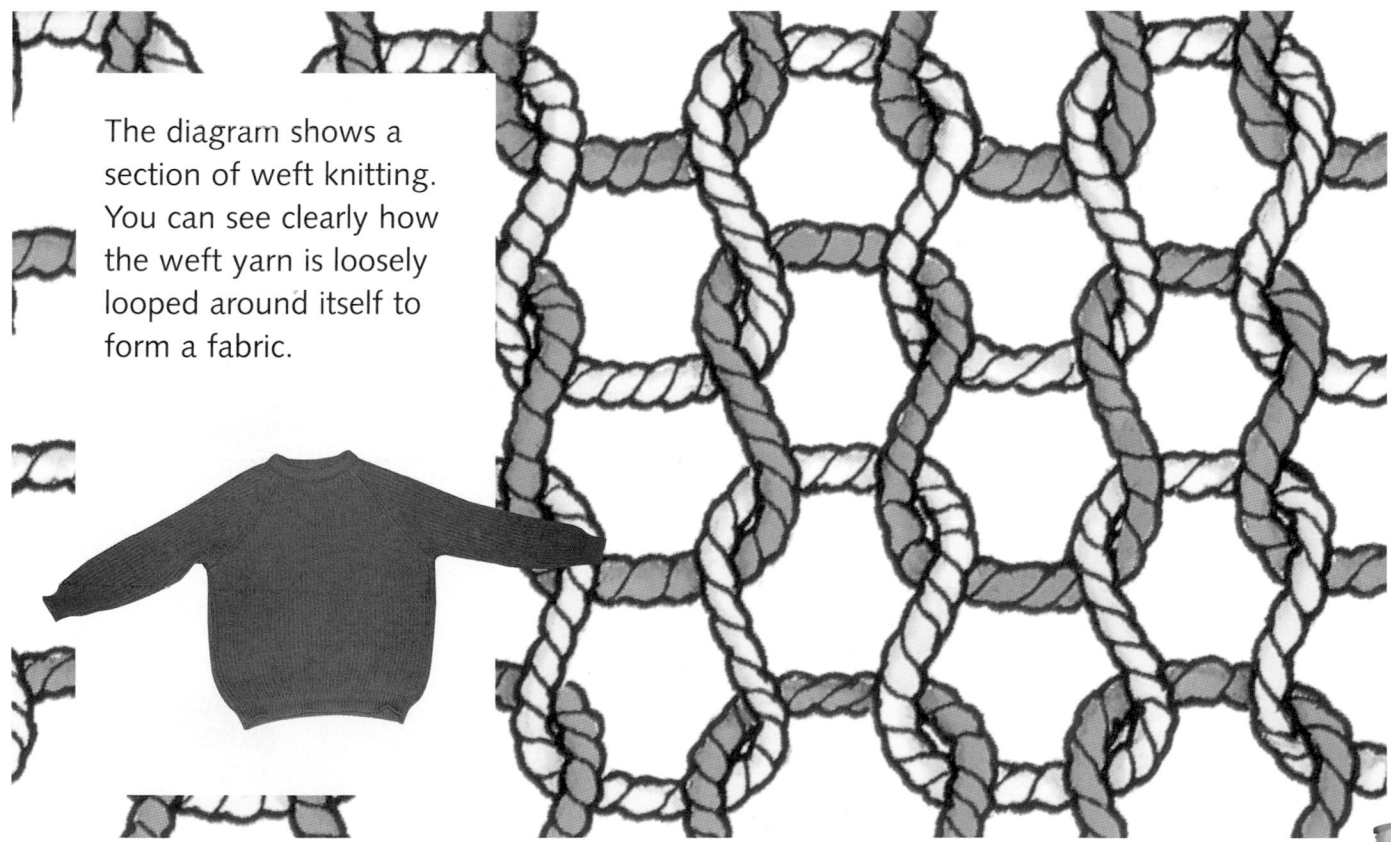

High speed knitting machines are now used for the manufacture of knitted materials.

The diagram shows a section of weft knitting. You can see clearly how the weft yarn is loosely looped around itself to form a fabric.

# DYEING AND PRINTING

The natural colour of fibres is off-white but fabrics can be dyed or printed to make them look more attractive. Dyes are coloured chemicals which stick to fibres. Natural dyes (from plants, vegetables, animals and certain minerals) have now been replaced almost entirely by man-made dyes.

In some cases yarn is dyed before weaving or knitting. Alternatively, print patterns and designs can be printed onto complete fabrics or clothes – producing similar items in a range of different colours.

A selection of water-soluble powder dyes

## Silk-screen printing

This traditional method of printing uses ink and a fine mesh of silk (or nylon). A different silk screen is made for each coloured ink used. To make the screen, the silk is treated with a chemical which stops ink passing through it. Some parts of the silk are left untreated to allow the ink to pass through. The first silk screen is placed on the fabric and green ink (1) is forced through parts of it using a squeegee (2). The yellow flowers are printed in a similar way using a second screen (3). By using a number of different screens, colourful and complicated patterns can be printed. Silk-screen printing can be used to decorate fabric and paper.

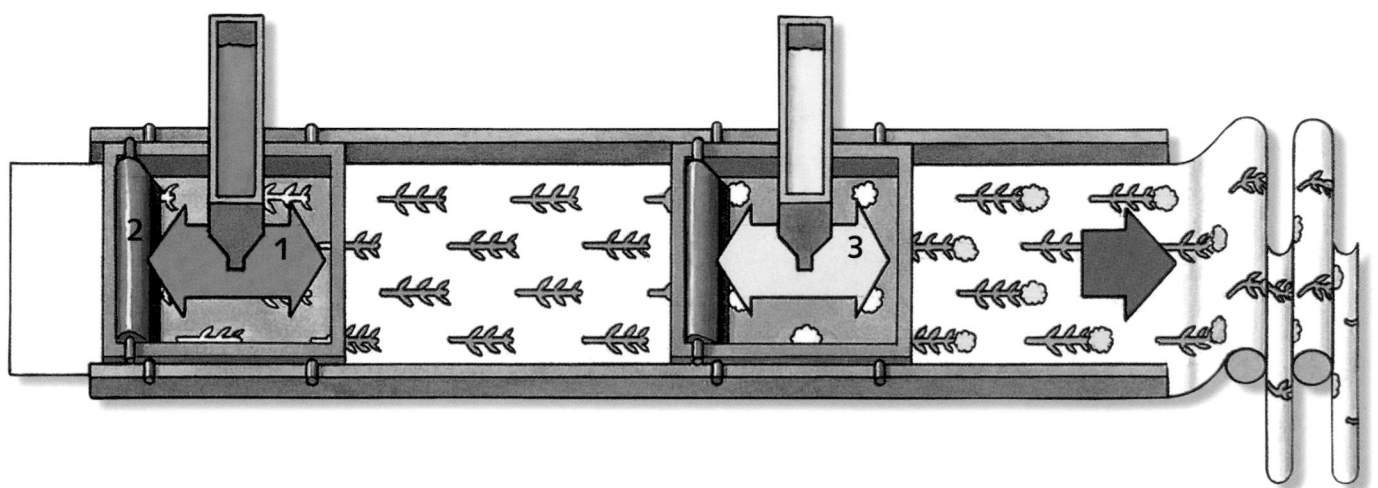

Dyes are used around the world to make brightly coloured cloth and clothing.

# FINISHING TOUCHES

Textiles made from natural fibres can be treated to give them different qualities. Chemicals can be added to make cloth colourfast or stain resistant. Cotton can be treated with caustic soda solution to make a glossy fabric, like silk. A chemical called chlorine can also be used to prevent fabrics from shrinking in the wash.

Wool fabrics can be treated with chemicals to protect them from being eaten by moth larvae, or to make woollens machine-washable. They can also be brushed to soften the fabric. The diagrams below show some of the ways in which woollen fabrics are treated to give them their final characteristics.

Tweed

## Improving comfort
Tweed and worsted are both strong and smooth fabrics. Their surface is raised by being pushed through prickly revolving drums. (left). This makes them more comfortable to wear (below).

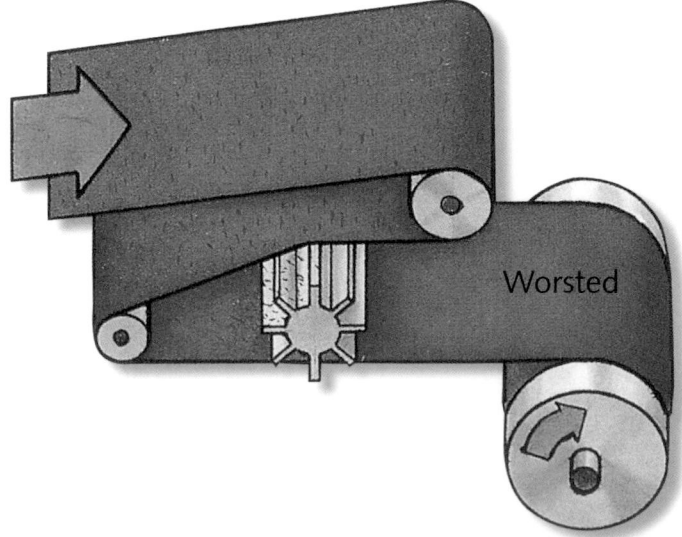

Worsted

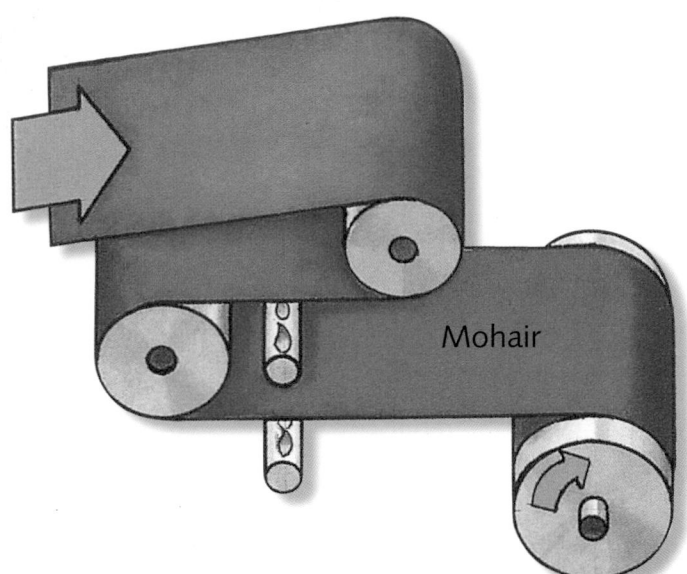

## Processing mohair

Mohair is a luxurious, long and strong fibre that comes from the fleece of the angora goat. It is a naturally soft fibre but it has a very 'hairy' surface. During processing, mohair is passed over a gas flame which burns off the longest hairs which would otherwise tickle when the fabric was worn.

Fabrics are steamed and pressed to smooth out creases and produce a glossy finish.

# TEXTILES AND THE FUTURE

Textiles are so important to our daily lives that it is not surprising that new artificial fibres and new ways of 'weaving' them together are constantly being developed.

Fabrics for tents and raincoats are coated in resin to make them waterproof; other fabrics like Gore-Tex allow moisture to pass out, while preventing rain from coming in. Stretchy Lycra sportswear uses new ways of twisting fibres together. Ultra-strong synthetic fibres are bonded together to make Kevlar – a tough, but very light fabric, used for bullet-proof clothing and certain sports gear.

Wetsuits are made from man-made fibres that are both waterproof and insulating.

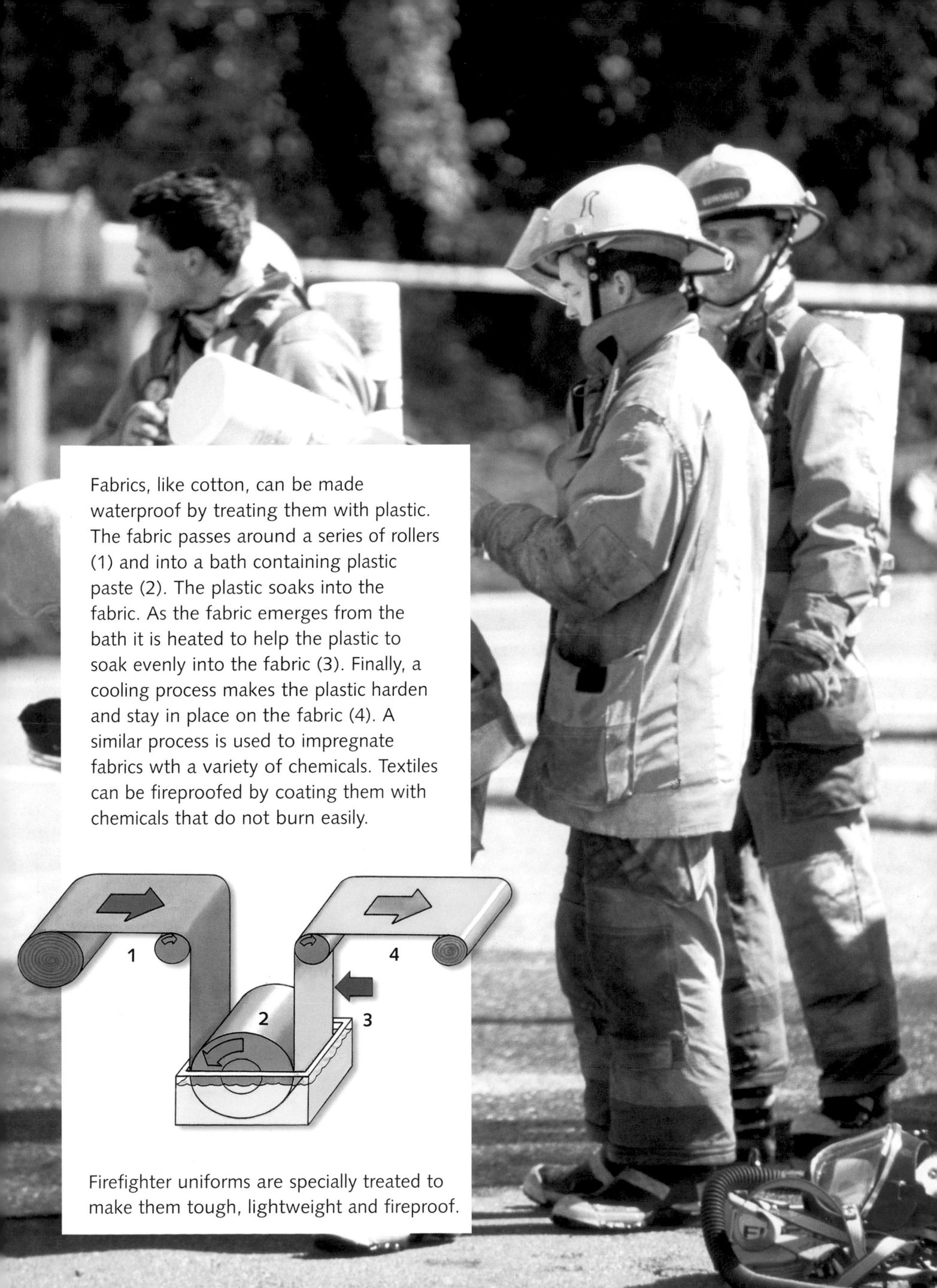

Fabrics, like cotton, can be made waterproof by treating them with plastic. The fabric passes around a series of rollers (1) and into a bath containing plastic paste (2). The plastic soaks into the fabric. As the fabric emerges from the bath it is heated to help the plastic to soak evenly into the fabric (3). Finally, a cooling process makes the plastic harden and stay in place on the fabric (4). A similar process is used to impregnate fabrics wth a variety of chemicals. Textiles can be fireproofed by coating them with chemicals that do not burn easily.

Firefighter uniforms are specially treated to make them tough, lightweight and fireproof.

# THE ENVIRONMENT

Textiles are a part of our everyday life, but the processes used to produce them can also have a damaging effect on our environment. We have come a long way in reducing the environmental impact of textiles with an established recycling industry, renewable sources of natural fibres and a reduction in the use of chemicals. But we still need to do a lot more to reduce the impact that the textile industry has on our planet.

### ◀ Pollution

When pesticides are applied to cotton fields, or sheeps' wool is treated to prevent disease, the chemicals used can harm wildlife and pollute fields and rivers nearby. Genetically modified crops, with a resistance to pests and disease, are now being developed to reduce the need for chemicals in textile production.

### ▶ Renewable sources

The coal and oil used to make some man-made fibres are in danger of running out. Scientists are looking at further sources of man-made fibres such as the cellulose found in natural plants like flax (right), hemp and straw. These plants can be specially grown and harvested on a regular basis.

## ◄ Wildlife

Clothing is the most common product of textiles, but other applications are often used in everyday life – like netting, string and cord. Some of these textiles can have a direct effect on wildlife. Sea birds and marine mammals can get caught in fishing nets, while other birds become tangled in awnings or football nets. If string or other ties are eaten they can harm an animal's intestines. String or twine can also cause damage if they get wrapped around an animal's foot or wing.

## ► Geotextiles

Scientists have recently developed textiles that can be used to make the disposal of waste products kinder to the environment. A woven biodegradable blanket is now used to line the bottom of landfill sites. This helps to contain the waste material whilst interacting naturally with the soil at the same time. Similar textiles can be used for drainage purposes and to reduce soil erosion.

## ◄ What you can do

Think before you throw your old clothes away! Many recycling centres now have a bank for textiles, such as clothing, curtains and bedding. These can be recycled to make paper, furniture and upholstery stuffings. Alternatively, you can take your clothes to a charity shop where they will help raise money and be put to good use. Don't forget that old rags can also be used as cleaning cloths around the home.

# TEXTILES AND THEIR USES

There is a wide variety of textiles to choose from. The table below shows where different textiles come from, how they are produced and what they are used for – everything from clothes to carpets.

The textile industry is largely concerned with the making of clothes. What types of fibres are you wearing? Are they natural or man-made, printed or dyed? As fashions change, different textiles become popular. Denim jeans are just one example of a successful fashion design made from cotton. Textiles are also used in household furnishings. Jute or hessian are used to back carpets, and cushions are stuffed with kapok.

| | Product | Where it comes from | Manufacturing method | Uses include |
|---|---|---|---|---|
| **ANIMAL** | Wool | Wool comes from sheep, goats, camels and llamas – all over the world. | The wool is sheared off, then combed and drawn out. Then it is spun or twisted. | Carpets, rugs, clothing, curtains, blankets, felt and upholstery. |
| | Silk | Silkworms raised in Japan, China, India, Bulgaria, France, Mexico and Turkey. | The silk threads of the silkworm cocoons are unwound to form a yarn. | Clothing, scarves, ties, lace, ribbon, bed linen, linings, fine upholstery and home furnishings. |
| **VEGETABLE** | Flax | Flax is grown in damp, cool climates in USSR, Belgium, France and the Netherlands. | The stalks of the plant go through several processes to produce useable fibres. | Tablecloths, towels, bed linen, clothing, fine upholstery and home furnishings. |
| | Cotton | Cotton is grown in the warm and moist regions of the world. | Cotton goes through several processes until the fibre can be spun. | Clothing, bed linen, home furnishings, towels, bags and medical dressings. |
| | Hemp | Hemp grows in warm regions of Asia, Europe and North America. | The stalks of the plant go through several processes to produce useable fibres. | Clothing, rope, twine, canvas, sacks, bags, sail cloth and home furnishings. |

| Product | Where it comes from | Manufacturing method | Uses include |
|---|---|---|---|
| **Jute** | Jute comes from tropical regions such as India or Pakistan. | The stalks of the plant go through several processes to produce useable fibres. | Rope, twine, sacks, hessian, mats and carpet backing. |
| **Ramie** | Ramie (grass cloth) is found in the warmer parts of China and Japan. | The stalks of the plant go through several processes to produce useable fibres. | Tablecloths, towels, home furnishings and bed linen. |
| **Kapok** | Kapok is grown in Java, Indonesia and southern parts of Asia. | The tree seed is processed to produce the white fluffy kapok. | Stuffing in upholstery, cushions and other home furnishings. |
| **Sisal** | Sisal grows in Eastern Africa, Java and tropical America. | The leaves are cultivated to produce the fibres. | Ropes, twine, sacks, carpets, rugs, mats and bags. |
| **Viscose** | Viscose rayon is mainly made from spruce trees. | Processed from cellulose and wood pulp. | Clothing, scarves, bags and nets. |
| **Lurex** | Lurex is made from aluminium mined mainly in South Africa. | The aluminium is coated with fabric. | Clothing, lace, ribbon, upholstery and home furnishings. |
| **Asbestos** | Asbestos is mined in South Africa, Java, tropical America, Canada and Italy. | It is taken from veins in various types of rocks. | Used for insulation and fireproof cloth but is known to be a hazard. |
| **Nylon** | Polyamides (nylon) are made from fossil fuels such as oil. | Polymerized – a chemical process that makes plastics – by heating. | Clothing, carpets, bedding, string, nets and rope. |
| **Polyester** | Polyesters (terylene) are made from fossil fuels. | Polymerized – a chemical process that makes plastics – by heating. | Clothing, stockings, linings, carpets, parachutes, hot air balloons and kites. |
| **Acrylic** | Acrylics (acrilan) made from fossil fuels. | Formed by dissolving chemicals. | Clothing, rugs, blankets, carpets and home furnishings. |
| **Modacrylic** | Modacrylics are made from fossil fuels. | Formed by dissolving chemicals. | Clothing, carpets, blankets and home furnishings. |

VEGETABLE

MINERAL

# TEXTILES TODAY

This map of the world shows where some of the most common natural fibres are produced. You will see that different fibres are produced in different parts of the world.

A country's climate has a lot to do with the plant or animal fibres it produces. For example, sheep do not breed well in very cold climates so you do not find wool being produced in the far north of Europe or in Canada. Cotton grows well in areas where there is a warm, wet growing season and a dry, warm picking season – such as in parts of the United States.

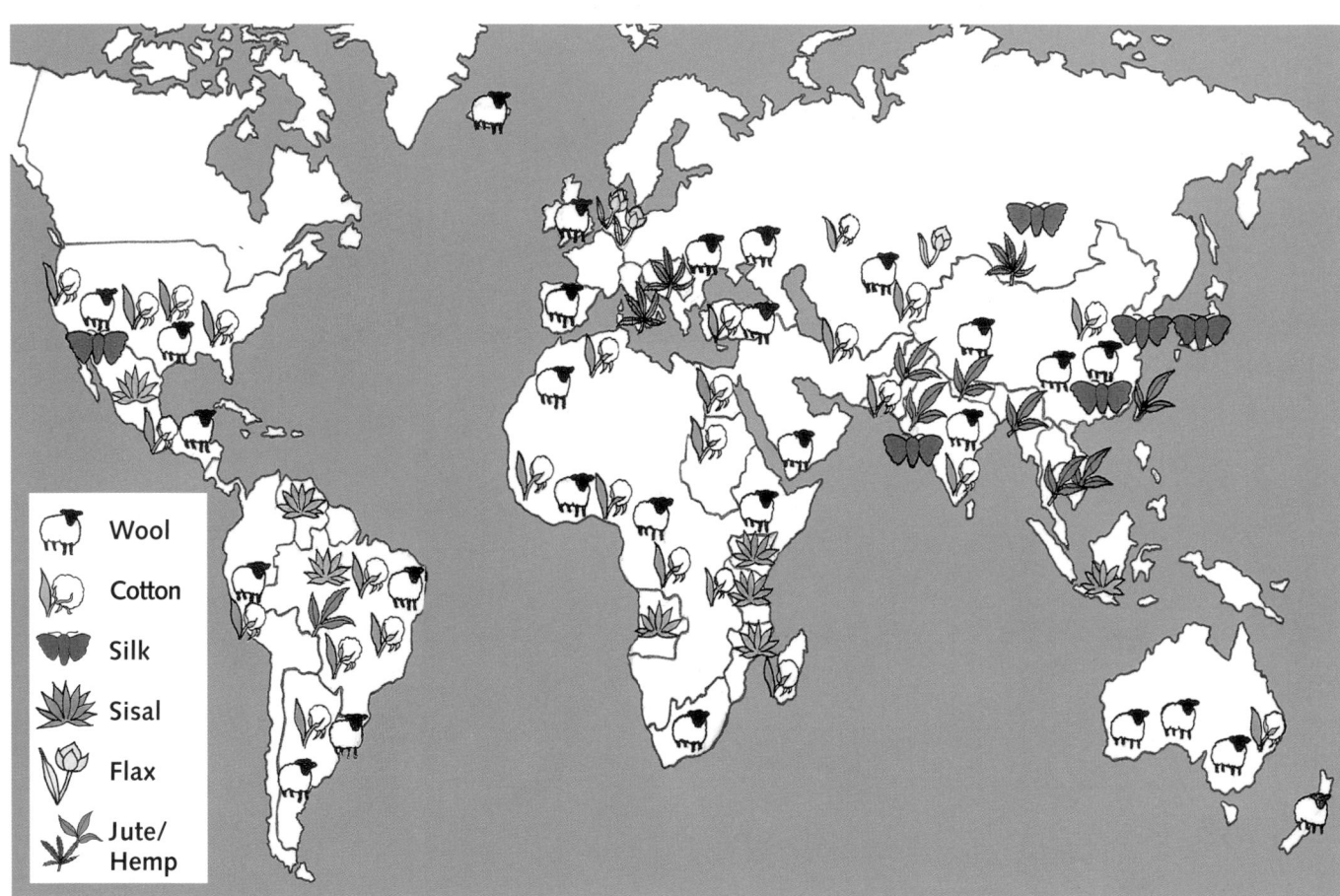

Wool
Cotton
Silk
Sisal
Flax
Jute/Hemp

The demand for a particular fibre also affects where it is produced. For example, the introduction of rayon and nylon in the 1930s caused the Chinese silk market to dwindle. Likewise, America is now the leading cotton producer because it can afford to buy machinery, fertilisers and pesticides and has developed its own genetically modified cotton. The only textile produced in any quantity in the UK is wool – the climate is too cold for plant fibres to grow well.

# GLOSSARY

**Bobbin**
A reel on which a thread is wound.

**Carding**
Preparing the fibres of cotton or wool for spinning by combing them.

**Cellulose**
A chemical found in wood and other plants that can be used to make fibres.

**Cocoon**
A silky protective coating made by insect larvae before they transform into an adult.

**Felting**
Making a fabric by pressing fibres together.

**Fibre**
Any hair or fine thread used for spinning into yarn.

**Filament**
Fine thread.

**Fleece**
The coat of wool that covers the body of a sheep or similar animal.

**Ginning**
Separating cotton fibres from cotton seeds.

**Knitting**
Making a fabric from yarn, using loops or stitches.

**Loom**
A machine used for weaving.

**Man-made fibre**
A material made artificially by a chemical reaction. Man-made fibres are also called 'synthetic fibres'.

**Roving**
Several slivers of fibres twisted together.

**Shuttle**
A box or stick which carries weft threads through the gap in the warp threads on a loom.

**Silk-screen printing**
A method of printing using a fine mesh of silk or nylon. Ink passes through the areas of silk which have not been covered by a special coating.

**Sliver**
Clean, straightened fibres.

**Spinneret**
A nozzle full of tiny holes, used for making fine threads of man-made fibres.

**Spinning**
Twisting fibres into yarn or forcing liquid through a small hole to make synthetic yarns.

**Textile**
Anything which is made from fibres or yarns. The fibres can be either man-made or natural.

**Thread**
A fine strand or fibre.

**Warp**
Threads in woven material that run lengthways.

**Weaving**
Forming a fabric by crossing yarns at right angles. Weaving is normally done on a machine called a loom.

**Weft**
Threads in woven material that run widthways.

**Worsted**
A fine, strong, tightly twisted yarn spun from combed wool – or the cloth made from this yarn.

**Yarn**
Fibres which have been spun together.

# INDEX